My First Pet Bilingual Library from the American Humane Association

Mi primer pajarito
My First Bird

AMERICAN HUMANE

Protecting Children & Animals Since 1877

Enslow Elementary
an imprint of
Enslow Publishers, Inc.
40 Industrial Road
Box 398
Berkeley Heights, NJ 07922
USA

http://www.enslow.com

Linda Bozzo

AMERICAN HUMANE

Protecting Children & Animals Since 1877

Founded in 1877, the American Humane Association is the oldest national organization dedicated to protecting both children and animals. Through a network of child and animal protection agencies and individuals, the American Humane Association develops policies, legislation, curricula, and training programs to protect children and animals from abuse, neglect, and exploitation. To learn how you can support the vision of a nation where no child or animal will ever be a victim of willful abuse or neglect, visit www.americanhumane.org, phone (303) 792-9900, or write to the American Humane Association at 63 Inverness Drive East, Englewood, Colorado, 80112-5117.

● ●

This book is dedicated to my husband and daughters, who never stop believing in me, and to pet lovers everywhere.

● ●

Enslow Elementary, an imprint of Enslow Publishers, Inc. Enslow Elementary® is a registered trademark of Enslow Publishers, Inc.

Bilingual edition copyright 2009 by Enslow Publishers, Inc. Originally published in English under the title *My First Bird* © 2008 by Enslow Publishers, Inc. Bilingual edition translated by Romina C. Cinquemani, edited by Susana C. Schultz of Strictly Spanish, LLC.

Library of Congress Cataloging-in-Publication Data

Bozzo, Linda.
[My first bird. Spanish & English]
Mi primer pajarito = My first bird / Linda Bozzo.
p. cm. — (My first pet bilingual library from the American Humane Association)
Added t.p. title: My first bird
Includes bibliographical references and index.
Summary: "Introduces young readers to the responsibilities of owning a bird, in English and Spanish"—Provided by publisher.
ISBN-13: 978-0-7660-3034-3
ISBN-10: 0-7660-3034-2
1. Cage birds—Juvenile literature. I. Title. II. Title: My first bird.
SF429.M58M6818 2009
636.6—dc22

2008004541

Printed in the United States of America

10 9 8 7 6 5 4 3 2 1

To Our Readers: We have done our best to make sure all Internet Addresses in this book were active and appropriate when we went to press. However, the author and the publisher have no control over and assume no liability for the material available on those Internet sites or on other Web sites they may link to. Any comments or suggestions can be sent by e-mail to comments@enslow.com or to the address on the back cover.

Every effort has been made to locate all copyright holders of material used in this book. If any errors or omissions have occurred, corrections will be made in future editions of this book.

♻ Enslow Publishers, Inc., is committed to printing our books on recycled paper. The paper in every book contains 10% to 30% post-consumer waste (PCW). The cover board on the outside of each book contains 100% PCW. Our goal is to do our part to help young people and the environment too!

Illustration Credits: Arco Images/Alamy, p. 15 top); courtesy of Larry DiMicco, pp. 21, 22; image100, pp. 9, 18, 27; Noel Hendrickson/ Masterfile, p. 3; Photodisc, p. 10; Pixtal, p. 7; Shutterstock, pp. 1, 4, 5, 6, 8, 11, 12, 13, 15 (bottom), 16, 17, 19 (top and bottom), 20, 23, 24, 25, 26, 28, 29, 30.

Cover Credits: Shutterstock.

Contents / Contenido

Wonderful Pets

Birds make wonderful pets. Just like you, they are smart. They like to play and are fun to watch. Bringing a new, **feathered** friend into your home can be exciting.

This book can help answer questions you may have about finding and caring for your new pet bird.

Mascotas maravillosas

Los pajaritos son excelentes mascotas. Al igual que tú, son muy inteligentes. Les gusta jugar y es divertido mirarlos. Traer un nuevo amiguito **emplumado** a tu hogar puede ser emocionante.

Este libro puede ayudarte a responder preguntas que pudieras tener acerca de cómo encontrar y cuidar a tu nuevo pajarito.

A Quaker Parrot

Un loro cuáquero

Parrots can make good pets.

Los periquitos pueden ser muy buenas mascotas.

What Kind of Bird Should I Get?

There are many kinds of birds to choose from. Some birds talk while others sing. Some birds are quiet. Birds come in many sizes. They come in many beautiful colors. Some birds can live a very long time. You will want to pick the perfect bird for you.

¿Qué clase de pajarito debo comprar?

Existen muchas clases de aves entre las cuales puedes elegir. Algunos pajaritos hablan, en tanto que otros cantan. Algunos son tranquilos. Hay pajaritos de todos los tamaños. También tienen hermosos colores. Algunos pajaritos pueden vivir mucho tiempo. Es conveniente que elijas el mejor pajarito para que sea tu mascota.

A purple-breasted red-headed Gouldian Finch

Un pinzón de Gould de pecho púrpura y cabeza roja

These pretty birds are red, yellow, and green.

Estos bonitos pajaritos son rojos, amarillos y verdes.

Where Should I Get a Pet Bird?

Ask a special bird **vet**, or animal doctor, where to get a bird. Other bird owners might also be glad to help. The bird you choose should be alert. Alert birds are lively and quick. This means they are healthy. An alert bird has been kept in a large, clean cage.

¿Dónde debo buscar un pajarito para mascota?

Consulta con un **veterinario** especialista en aves, o un doctor de animales, cuál es el mejor lugar para comprar un pajarito. Otros dueños de pajaritos se alegrarán al poder ayudarte. El pajarito que elijas debe verse vivaz. Los pajaritos que se ven vivaces son saludables y rápidos. Esto significa que están sanos. Un pajarito vivaz ha sido mantenido en una jaula grande y limpia.

Make sure the bird you buy is alert.

Asegúrate de que el pajarito que compres esté alerta.

A Lovebird
Un periquito

Ask a bird doctor to help you find the right pet bird.

Consulta a un veterinario especialista en aves para que te ayude a encontrar a tu mascota adecuada.

What Will I Need to Buy for My Bird?

Your bird will want a cage it can call home. The cage you choose should have room for your bird. It needs room in its cage to flap its wings and fly.

Birds like perches.

¿Qué deberé comprar para mi pajarito?

Tu pajarito necesitará una jaula que sea su hogar. La jaula que elijas debe tener lugar suficiente para tu pajarito. Él necesita espacio dentro de la jaula para poder mover las alas y volar.

A los pajaritos les gustan las perchas.

perch

percha

Birds like perches.

A los pajaritos les gustan las perchas

10

This African Grey
Parrot likes its
toy ball.

A este loro gris
africano le
gusta su pelota
de juguete.

Find a cage that is easy to clean. The cage should be safe and made just for pet birds.

Your bird will need a feeder and a water dish.

Do not forget, birds like to climb. They also like to jump. There should be at least two perches inside your bird's cage. Perches come in different shapes.

Toys can bring fun into your bird's cage. Some favorite bird toys are bells, swings, and mirrors. Birds also like toys they can peck and chew.

Consigue una jaula que sea sencilla para limpiar. La jaula debe ser segura y debe estar hecha especialmente para pajaritos.

Tu pajarito necesitará un recipiente con alimento y otro con agua (bebedero).

No olvides que a los pajaritos les gusta trepar. También les encanta saltar. Por eso debe haber, como mínimo, dos perchas atravesadas dentro de la jaula. Las perchas vienen en diferentes tamaños.

Los juguetes pueden agregar diversión a la jaula de tu pajarito. Algunos de los juguetes favoritos de los pajaritos son las campanas, los columpios y los espejos. También les gustan los juguetes que pueden picotear y masticar.

It is best to put a few different toys in a
bird's cage.

Es conveniente colocar algunos juguetes
diferentes dentro de la jaula del pajarito.

Where Should I Keep My New Pet?

Birds do not like to be alone. Your new pet will want to be near you. Place the cage in a safe place that is not too noisy. Be sure to keep your bird in a place where it will not get too warm or too cold. Keep your bird away from candles, smoke, and cleaning products. These can hurt your pet. Ask your vet if you are not sure about where to place your pet bird.

Keep an eye on your bird if you take it out of its cage.

¿En qué lugar de la casa deberé tener a mi pajarito?

A los pajaritos no les gusta estar solos. Tu nueva mascota querrá estar cerca de ti. Coloca la jaula en un lugar seguro que no sea muy ruidoso. Asegúrate de mantener a tu pajarito en un lugar donde no haga demasiado frío ni demasiado calor. Mantén a tu pajarito lejos de velas, humo y productos de limpieza. Todo esto podría dañar a tu mascota. Consulta al veterinario en caso que no estés seguro acerca del mejor lugar para colocar la jaula de tu mascota.

Siempre vigila bien a tu pajarito si lo sacas de su jaula.

Take time to make your bird's cage a fun place to live.

Tómate el tiempo necesario para hacer de la jaula de tu pajarito un lugar divertido para él.

Birds like to play together.

A los pajaritos les gusta jugar juntos.

What Should I Feed My Bird?

Birds are like people. They like different foods. Some birds eat fruits and vegetables. Some eat seeds or **pellets**. Find which foods are best for your bird.

Give your bird fresh water to drink every day.

¿Con qué debo alimentar a mi pajarito?

Los pajaritos son como las personas. Les gustan diferentes alimentos. Algunos pajaritos comen frutas y vegetales. Algunos comen semillas o **pellets**. Averigua qué alimentos son los mejores para tu pajarito.

Dale de beber a tu pajarito agua fresca todos los días.

A Macaw

Un guacamayo

This bird enjoys seeds.

A este pajarito le encantan
las semillas.

Western Rosella

Perico carigualdo

How Should I Clean My Bird?

Birds like to keep clean. Some like to splash in a dish of water in the bottom of their cage. Some like a shower of warm water from a spray bottle.

¿Cómo debo limpiar a mi pajarito?

A los pajaritos les gusta estar limpios. A algunos les agrada chapotear en un plato con agua, en el fondo de su jaula. A otros les gustan las duchas de agua tibia con un rociador.

Your vet will make sure your bird is clean and healthy.

El veterinario de tu mascota se asegurará de que tu pajarito esté limpio y saludable.

18

Keep your bird
clean and it
will be happy.

Mantén limpio
a tu pajarito y
él será feliz.

19

How Often Should I Clean the Cage?

Birds can be messy. Change the paper in the bottom of the cage every day. Throw away old food and water. Wash the cage, once a week, with special soap made just for birds.

Make sure you change your bird's food and water every day.

¿Con qué frecuencia debo limpiar la jaula?

Los pajaritos pueden ser sucios. Cambia el papel del fondo de la jaula todos los días. Bota el alimento y el agua del día anterior. Lava la jaula, una vez por semana, con jabón especial hecho sólo para pajaritos.

Asegúrate de cambiar el alimento y el agua de tu pajarito todos los días.

A Chinese White-eye

Ojiblanco chino

20

When you clean your bird's cage, check its droppings. Ask an adult for help.

Cuando limpies la jaula de tu pajarito, revisa sus heces. Pídele ayuda a un adulto.

Make sure you change your bird's food and water every day.

Asegúrate de cambiar la comida y el agua de tu pajarito todos los días.

These birds enjoy their perches.

A estos pajaritos les encantan
sus perchas.

Gouldian Finches

Pinzones de Gould

How Will I Know If My Bird Is Sick?

With good care most pet birds will stay healthy. But there are times when birds get sick.

¿Cómo sabré si mi pajarito está enfermo?

Con los cuidados necesarios, la mayoría de los pajaritos vivirán sanos. Pero en ciertas ocasiones, los pajaritos pueden enfermarse.

Happy, healthy birds are both beautiful and fun.

Los pajaritos felices y sanos son hermosos y divertidos.

Look closely at your birds each day
to make sure they are healthy.

Mira con atención a
tus pajaritos todos los
días para asegurarte
de que estén sanos.

Watch for changes in your bird's droppings. A sick bird may hang its head. It may also have trouble perching. Check that your bird is eating and drinking. If you think your bird might be sick, see your vet.

Revisa si se producen cambios en las heces de tu pajarito. Un pajarito enfermo podría dejar su cabeza colgando. También podría tener dificultades para posarse sobre su percha. Revisa que tu pajarito coma y beba. Si crees que tu mascota podría estar enferma, llévala al veterinario.

A clean cage leads to a happy bird!

¡Una jaula limpia guarda un pajarito feliz!

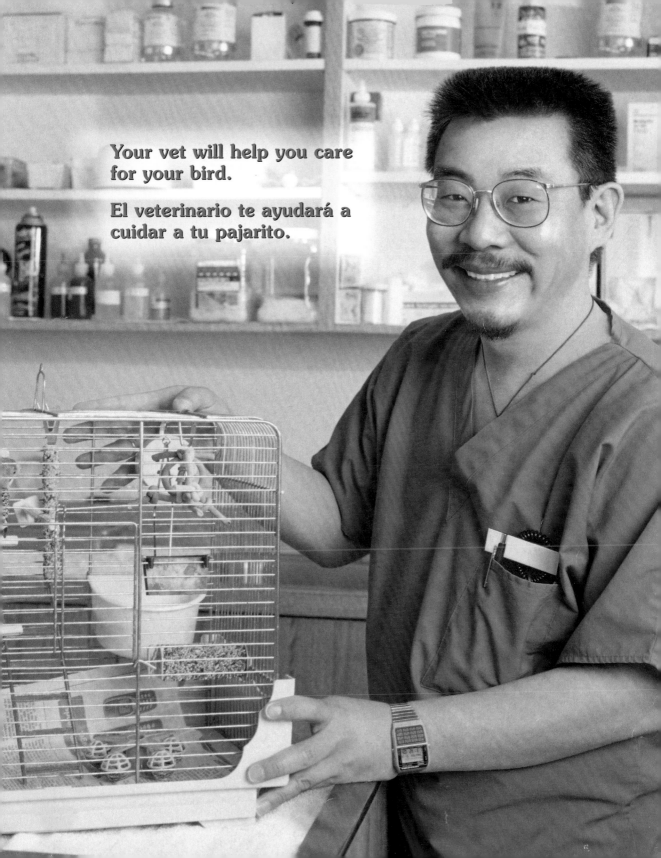

Your vet will help you care for your bird.

El veterinario te ayudará a cuidar a tu pajarito.

You and Your Feathered Friend

Give your bird time to get used to its new home. Be gentle. Love and care for your bird every day. Your bird will be your feathered friend for many years.

Tú y tu amigo emplumado

Dale tiempo a tu pajarito para que se adapte a su nuevo hogar. Sé dulce con él. Demuéstrale afecto y cuídalo todos los días. Tu pajarito será tu amigo emplumado durante muchos años.

Cockatiels

Cockatiels

Parakeets

Periquitos

Words to Know

feathered—Having feathers. A bird is feathered.

pellets—A special type of food that is small and round in shape.

vet—Vet is short for veterinarian, a doctor who takes care of animals.

Palabras a conocer

emplumado—Que tiene plumas. Un pajarito es una criatura emplumada.

los pellets—Un tipo especial de alimento que es pequeño y tiene forma redonda.

el veterinario—Un médico que cura animales.

Learn More
Más para aprender

BOOKS / LIBROS

In English / En inglés

Blackaby, Susan. *A Bird For You; Caring for Your Bird.* Minneapolis, Minn.: Picture Window Books, 2003.

Frost, Helen. *Parrots.* Minneapolis, Minn.: Capstone Press, 2002.

Howard, Fran. *Parrots: Colorful Birds.* Minneapolis, Minn.: Capstone Press, 2005.

In Spanish / En español

Durant, Alan. *Pajarín vuela al Sur.* Grand Rapids, Mich.: School Specialty Publishing, 2005.

INTERNET ADDRESSES / DIRECCIONES DE INTERNET

In English / En inglés

American Humane Association
  <http://www.americanhumane.org>

The American Society for the Prevention of Cruelty to Animals
  <http://www.animaland.org>

Index

Índice